Basking Sharks

BY LAURA HAMILTON WAXMAN

AMICUS HIGH INTEREST • AMICUS INK

Amicus High Interest and Amicus Ink are imprints of Amicus
P.O. Box 1329, Mankato, MN 56002
www.amicuspublishing.us

Library of Congress Cataloging-in-Publication Data
Names: Waxman, Laura Hamilton, author.
Title: Basking sharks / by Laura Hamilton Waxman.
Description: Mankato, MN : Amicus High Interest is an imprint
 of Amicus, [2017] | Audience: K to grade 3._ | Includes
 bibliographical references and index.
Identifiers: LCCN 2015033030| ISBN 9781607539742
 (library binding) | ISBN 9781681520872 (pbk.) | ISBN
 9781681510088 (ebook)
Subjects: LCSH: Basking shark–Juvenile literature. | Sharks–
Juvenile literature.
Classification: LCC QL638.95.C37 W388 2017 | DDC
 597.3–dc23
LC record available at http://lccn.loc.gov/2015033030

Editor: Wendy Dieker
Series Designer: Kathleen Petelinsek
Book Designer: Aubrey Harper
Photo Researchers: Derek Brown and Rebecca Bernin

Photo Credits: Alex Mustard/Nature Picture Library/
Corbis cover; FLPA/Andrew Mason/FLPA/Corbis 5;
Alex Mustard/2020VISION/Alamy 6-7; Alex Mustard/
Nature Picture Library/Corbis 9; Nature Picture Library/
Alamy 10; NaturePL/NaturePL/Superstock 13; Alex
Mustard/2020VISION/Nature Picture Library/Corbis 14;
Nature Picture Library/Alamy 16-17; Patrick Lyne/Flickr 18;
Martin Strmiska/Alamy 21; David Hastilow/Alamy 22; Jeff
Rotman/Alamy 25; Raymond Kleboe/Stringer/Getty 26; Wild
Wonders of Europe/ Sá/Nature Picture Library/Corbis 29

Printed in the United States of America.

HC 10 9 8 7 6 5 4 3 2 1
PB 10 9 8 7 6 5 4 3 2 1

Table of Contents

Is That a Shark?

It's springtime. You're standing on the beach, looking out at the ocean. Then you see it. A gray triangle sticks out of the water. It's a **fin**! And it belongs to a huge fish. Is it a great white shark? No! It's even bigger! Then you see the wide, yawning mouth. You can relax. It's a basking shark.

A fin sticking out of the water could mean danger. This time, it's a harmless basking shark.

Is this shark yawning? No! It's getting food. A basking shark gets food with its mouth wide open. Water flows in as the shark swims. It flows through the sharp **gill rakers** and out of the **gills**. The water is full of food. The gill rakers are like the teeth of a comb. They **filter** the food out of the water.

Tiny plants and animals get trapped in the shark's mouth as it swims.

The basking shark's gills do more than trap food. The gills also help them breathe underwater. The gills take in oxygen as the water passes through them. But look at the basking shark's gills. They are long and wide. They stretch from the top of its head to the bottom.

 What do basking sharks eat?

The basking shark's gills are much bigger than the gills on other fish and sharks.

 They eat zooplankton. These are tiny plants and animals that live in the ocean.

The sunlight creates a pattern
on the light and dark colors
of the giant basking shark.

 What is the biggest fish in the world?

Big Fish

Basking sharks are the world's second biggest fish. They can be more than 32 feet (10 m) long. That's longer than five grown men laid end to end.

Most basking sharks are gray or brown in color. Others look almost black. Many have white spots too. The spots are under the head and on the belly.

 It's another shark. It's called the whale shark.

Like all sharks, a basking shark's body is made to swim. But this shark glides slowly through the water. It uses its whole body to sway back and forth. Strong fins help too. The tail fin helps push the shark forward. Two side fins help it steer. Two back fins keep it steady. Fins under its body help the shark change directions.

This swishing tail is made to push a huge basking shark through the water.

Tiny fish have a hard time getting away from a basking shark's gaping mouth.

 Do basking sharks have teeth?

This basking shark is hungry. Time to find some food! The shark needs a lot of this food for its big body. It spends its days finding food in the ocean. Basking sharks spend much of their time at the surface of the ocean. The warm water at the surface is the best place for them to find food.

Yes! They have hundreds of small teeth in their mouths. But they don't use them to eat. Scientists are not sure why they have teeth.

Having Babies

Basking sharks mostly live alone. But they pair up to **mate**. First, a male and female shark meet in the water. Then they get to know each other. They swim side by side. They nudge each other. They even bite each other's fins. They are sending a message. It says, "Let's get together!"

Two basking sharks come together to mate.

This shark pup knew how to find food as soon as it was born.

 How many pups are born at a time?

New sharks begin to grow inside the female shark. These new sharks are inside eggs. The eggs hatch inside the mother after one to three years. Then the mother gives birth to baby sharks. The baby sharks are called pups. The mother shark's job is done. She swims away. Now the pups must take care of themselves.

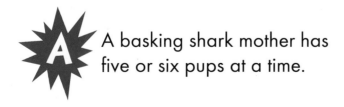 A basking shark mother has five or six pups at a time.

Staying Alive in the Ocean

Being big keeps these sharks safe. Adult basking sharks don't have any **predators**. Predators are animals that hunt and eat other animals. Young basking sharks aren't as lucky as the adults. They must watch out for large sharks. Big sharks hunt and eat basking shark pups.

Hammerhead sharks hunt all kinds of fish. Watch out shark pups!

These sharks swim near England.
When it gets cold, they will move
to warm water.

The biggest danger is hunger. Basking sharks must always look for food. They find the most food in the warm months. What happens when it gets cold? How can these sharks find enough food?

Basking sharks **migrate** to find more food. They swim to warmer waters. Sometimes they swim across the ocean.

Basking Sharks and People

Scientists work to study basking sharks. They attach tags to basking sharks. The tags send information to the scientists. They can see how deep the sharks dive. They can see where the sharks swim. Scientists can see how long sharks stay near the beach. They can see when they swim across the ocean. Scientists hope to learn more about how basking sharks live.

Scientists attach these tags to basking sharks to gather information.

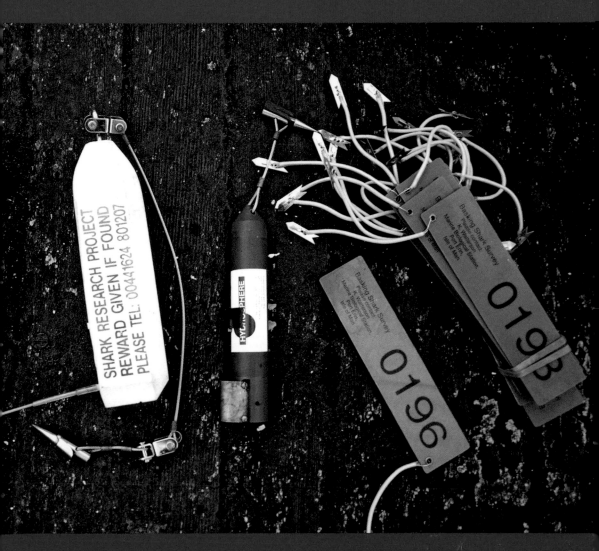

Basking sharks were once hunted in great numbers. This photo shows a Scottish shark hunter in 1946.

 Why are basking sharks easy to hunt?

People once hunted many of these sharks. They were easy to catch. People used the sharks' meat for food. They used other body parts for medicine and makeup. People in Asia still hunt basking sharks. They use the fins to make soup. But basking sharks have been hunted too much. Now there are not as many in the ocean.

 These sharks are not afraid of humans. They don't swim away when fishing boats get near.

Basking sharks are **endangered** in some places. That means they could die out. People are trying to help. In many countries, they have stopped hunting these sharks. They are also learning more about how the sharks live. They want to protect them better. Then these big animals can stay safe in the ocean.

Divers take pictures of basking sharks. They learn more so we can protect these giant fish.

Glossary

endangered In danger of dying out.

filter To trap something passing or flowing through.

fin Body parts that help a fish swim.

gill Body parts an animal uses to breathe.

gill rakers Sharp body parts in gills that trap food floating in water.

mate To come together to make babies.

migrate To travel a long distance from one place to another.

predator An animal that hunts other animals.

zooplankton Tiny sea creatures.